ANOTHER MISSED CONNECTION

Another Missed Connection

A collection of poems
by
DANIEL SENSER

Adelaide Books
New York / Lisbon
2020

ANOTHER MISSED CONNECTION
A collection of poems
By Daniel Senser

Copyright © by Daniel Senser
Cover design © 2020 Adelaide Books

Published by Adelaide Books, New York / Lisbon
adelaidebooks.org

Editor-in-Chief
Stevan V. Nikolic

All rights reserved. No part of this book may be reproduced in any manner whatsoever without written permission from the author except in the case of brief quotations embodied in critical articles and reviews.

For any information, please address Adelaide Books
at info@adelaidebooks.org
or write to:
Adelaide Books
244 Fifth Ave. Suite D27
New York, NY, 10001

ISBN: 978-1-951896-32-4

Printed in the United States of America

For Chayim

Contents

Another Missed Connection   *11*

Beauty   *12*

Phalangeal Advancement   *13*

Antediluvian Depths   *14*

Grave Digger   *15*

Adornment   *16*

Basement Bar   *17*

Puncturing Beauty   *18*

The Cry   *19*

The Stoker   *20*

Fantasia   *21*

To My First and Only Love   *22*

Mania   *23*

The Reaping   *24*

Shadow Song   *25*

Shadow Song #2 *27*

Shadow Song #3 *28*

Shadow Song #8 *29*

Shadow Song #9 *30*

Bottled Lightning *32*

The Saint on Top of the Mountain *33*

Gift of Pleasure *35*

Driving While Intoxicated *36*

Let It Be Said *37*

Peony Song *38*

Beethoven in a Storm *40*

The Fruit *41*

Haiku *42*

The Vixen *43*

The Color Blue *44*

Worm on a Hook *45*

Wake or Sleep *46*

Little-Known Facts About the Great Philosophers *47*

Eternally *49*

Conscience Absentium *50*

Sestet *51*

ANOTHER MISSED CONNECTION

Consumed by Flame **52**

Child of the Night Sky **53**

The Wound of Time **54**

Tonight, We Dance **55**

Elegiac Romance **57**

Sanctuary of the Black Moon **58**

A Drunkard Thinks **60**

Dawn **61**

Two Songbirds **62**

Pin Drop **64**

Swallow the Night **65**

Prayer **66**

On a Night Spent Dancing with a Vestal Virgin **68**

Typhoon **69**

Upon Seeing a Starlet in the Street **70**

Phantoms **71**

Jewish Humor **72**

Ode to Watermelon **74**

Desert Scene **75**

Changes **76**

Meeting Tolstoy **77**

The Lunatic's Howl **79**

Another Missed Connection

Our eyes met. All the colors of the world
bled together as in a child's painting,
or rather, God's masterpiece cheerfully
smeared by the child Eros.

(We can't scold him because we can't catch him.)

Still decipherable in the mess—two dark eyes
filled with fire and music.
The faun plays his fife in those eyes
and I, the poet, open my mouth to sing.

Oh, mirror of my soul!
The hot breath of fate has fogged you over
and before I can cast the lure of my song
into that silver pond filled with your longing,
you are gone! and my reflection is all that remains.

Beauty

The wind blows the cherry blossoms into the river,
where they are carried off by the current downstream—
perfect pink punctuation for the long flowing sentence
that yearns for the certainty of its period, the sea.
I watch the cherry tree shake like a rueful mother
saying goodbye to her beloved children.
She knows their healthy pink glow will not last
without her. She knows that the river carries them
to their graves. And yet, I cannot help but feel thankful
for this wondrous sacrifice, this theft by wind,
this deceitful ushering by river towards death.
I can forgive the cruel fate of all things beautiful,
and be thankful for beauty's inevitable return.

Phalangeal Advancement

The innocent and charming hysteria of my eyes
Served nicely as a diversion for my hand
Which rose up like the tide upon the sand
Of the inner portion of her stubbly thigh.
Before I could reach the cavern
Carved out in the underside of her short black skirt,
She cried out, "Don't!"
And as the sea follows Poseidon's commands,
So my hand was halted for the moment.
"Trust me," I said, sounding more like a boy than a man,
"This hand is pure as the guitarist's upon the strings—
Let me tune your soul to your own best liking,
And to mine, with this hand."
She lay back, eyes closed, smiling.
The sea rushed in, filling the cavern,
Which, for the briefest of moments,
Teemed with the life that I wanted for her.

Antediluvian Depths

My shadow struck the earth and shattered
into a million butterflies at dawn.
Darkness immersed itself in an ocean of light
and found treasures there
that reflected back the stars.
I have wept such that my tears have risen up
in a cloud of mist that veiled me
shielded me from the eyes
of those whose cups I would fill
and make drunk on the sweet nectar of my song.
The cloud lifts, and, now with
the grace of a once-hidden beauty revealed,
my voice takes over where my tears left off.

Whose tears are these that mix with my own?
This question hangs like the sun—a vision
unattainable by the eyes—over my head,
and my every breath tells a story that began
in the antediluvian depths, where love met hate
and day met night, and made peace with one another
before creating life.

Grave Digger

You won't find the Devil here
Amongst the clay and the worms
And the rock, nor the ache in the back
Nor the sweat of the brow.
The Devil makes no deals
In this field—fallow, and dry as bone.
My eyes never leave my work.
The only soul the Devil has to gain here
Is his own. Here, where the earth
Is pristine as death, I labor as a lost man
Will labor to find his home.
No rest for fear of idleness.
No dreams in labor will be born.
Naught but my soul will be saved.
Let this hole that I dig serve as a grave
For my body when I die,
And let my soul in its purity proliferate
Like starlight through these endless skies.

Adornment

Naked, she needed no adornment
Except for my body.

The garden in her eyes grew lush
Under the sunlight of my own.

Together, we constructed many shapes
Till, exhausted, we collapsed into the humid jungle

Of our united oblivion.

Basement Bar

We conversed in the midnight code
Of drunkenness
And my mind droned
As we drank greedy draughts of moonlight ale.
A life's worth of sin
In a night's worth of drinking
in this subterranean tavern—a granite hell.
Now edging toward oblivion, I can hear you murmuring
Trying to call me back
Like a vesper bell.
The cackled laughter full of death
Is the last line of defense I have
Between me and vacant slumber.
Tomorrow may never happen is all I think,
And maybe it's just as well.
In this place that could be a mausoleum
Full of mad and raucous dead,
My bibulous mind fills with drunken shadows
And like a weeping angel, I hold my head.

Puncturing Beauty

I was struck dumb
by the billion-flashbulb paparazzi
in her eyes.

My shutters closed
and I was left with a dual image:
the one, a drama of her restraint—
placid beauty, like the moon's undisturbed
reflection in a lake.
The second, her dissipation into comedy,
a muted smile, developing
like a slow breeze in early Autumn,
on her face.

Winter will be here soon.
I will adhere to the risings and fallings
of the moon.
Looking up at the starry sky
the universe an inverse
of her eye, in the surrounding mind
I am a cancerous speck now,
disregarded except for
(if my hunch is right)
A single smile.

The Cry

The cry rings out over the darkened streets
Nothing can silence the silence that stands
As solid proof for a pain that has no beginning
And no end.
Somewhere in the shadows a man is recollecting his burden—
The broken shards of a mirror
Which reflect everything
Except the truth which is hidden
Behind his searching eyes.

The Stoker

I want to be the stoker of your fire
And the smoke that rises through your chimney.
I want to be the dream in your dream catcher,
The clapper inside your bell
That announces the call to prayer each morning.
I want my tongue to be the one
That reads the prayer from your open book.
I want to be the beast inside your cage
Pacing and roaring, devouring the flesh you give.
I want to be the minion surrounding
Your sacred ark, be the one who opens
Your curtain, revealing the sacred light.
I want to be the knowledge of your flesh,
The fuel that makes your fire ignite.
I want my rod to be the one that casts your lure
Into an ocean of delight.
I want to be the sun in your day and the moon in your night.
I want to be the earth beneath you,
The heavens above.
I want this song to wrap its wings around us
And squeeze us so tight we have no choice
But to make love.

Fantasia

Long ago I made my peace
with the cunning in the fortune teller's eyes,
the brisk current of the coming days,
and the madman inside me flailing with rage
against my decision to try and be kind.

Despite this, there are nights when I slip away
from the slimy grasp of my typical self
and seize the night as a child,
squeeze out the moon like a big silver sponge,
drink the moonshine
and go skipping over the hills, drunk and wild.

And on these nights I pluck a star from the sky
like a plasmatic apple succulent with supernova juices
that flow like the cosmos when my teeth crack its skin.

And so (mostly on full-moon nights)
I spin down the black hole of fantasy,
feel the freedom of a warped time and space.
I see my lover's face in every photon,
feel the presence of her dark matter
everywhere.

I find myself drifting away into the dark sky
in care-free oblivion, carried upward by
a heavy sigh, headed to the most distant star—
easy as forgetting, weightless as a dream.

To My First and Only Love

My soul was damned, a bastard-child
Unclaimed by the world,
But you lulled the Devil
From my heart.
You became the religion
That gave my fear a name.
I shed the blood of a thousand holy dreams
Upon your altar. In your covenant,
I was saved.
But now that you are gone,
The Devil has come back.
I set fire to your temple
And cover myself
In the ashes.
Outcast, hard of heart,
I fight this war against myself.
Retreating from love,
Though it surrounds me on every side,
I bury the cry that is sure to come
And the bittersweet tears with it.

Mania

Each moment is filled to the brim
With the lasting resonation
Of circular-breathing bells.
Time lapses into her silk-upholstered divan
And watches with languid eyes
The celestial dance of myself within myself
In this little room where silence makes itself go mad
Whenever silence dares to arise (and it does, without fail.
Every time). Sun-bathed or moon-struck dumb,
Sleepless, no sheep to count, they are in the field,
I count the kisses on the back of my hand.
There is no disordering the monstrous order of it all!
Every cell in its place, still day three and I am awake.
Coffee to placate my desire. Caffeine to destroy my reason.
Thoughts are holding a demonstration in my brain—
Vague thoughts, the ones I have ignored all these years.
My eyes, windows into my soul, shudder.
Impossible to know which way is in, which way is out,
Except by the flow of tears.
(Follow that river!) Downstream was promised paradise.
Convulsing becomes remembering,
Remembering becomes release.
Bury your face in the pillow,
Let it be a grave for all this madness.
With tears spent, dreamless sleep comes,
And you awaken, your soul as if reborn.

The Reaping

Here where I lie, watching your body rise
Into the new day, need and desire
Become one and the same.
I feast my eyes, for my lust is good,
Good as any hunger that bid me eat.
Yours are the fruits of the celestial garden
Where I have sown all my life
All my life, and now, as my hands
Explore your body, as if searching for a grip
To lift my soul out of the abyss,
Now that the light hits your cheek
So gently, now let us share
In the reaping.

Shadow Song

I speak my love in the language of shadows.
In the light of the moon, I have shed the soulless skin
Of my past, and stood, a clock gone wild,
In and out of time.
My patience is a starving hawk
Circling the sky above a desolate plane,
Zeroing in on a tiny speck of dust, and wearing thin.
Immovable darkness! I am saving my last breath
To take you in.
This free-fall through life
Has left me stupefied. The light above me is growing dim.
Neither darkness nor light
But in the space between I live.
Perplexed, the shadows dance in panic,
Their mindless hunt for the night begins.
Zoroaster's key is in the lock,
Keen on epiphany. Horrible gusts of shadow
Rant and rave through the open door.
Lost in their masquerade, I feel my pulse
Beginning to slow.
The cold hand of time is wrapped around my throat,
My breath is slowly leaving me.
The strings of my gold harp are snapping,
I have but a few left to play,
And the music, though more refined,
Grows less diversiform every day.
In the landscape of my body and soul,

There exist many graves.
I visit the one that marks my birth,
Not as one who remembers,
But as one who seeks to understand
What was lost before his time.
Shadows merge and the bells begin to chime.
The bells stir and homogenize the night,
Their vibrations churn the very earth,
And so the grave of my birth is churned.
The song of death permeates up through my feet
And into my mind. The drum of night is being played.
The whole universe is a doorway
That opens upon a mirror.
With a single stroke death shatters the glass,
Revealing...No one can say.
Breath eternal, neither the beginning nor the end,
Inhale, exhale, revolving around each other,
Becoming one.
Now these words dissolve,
Now these words have meaning: a disappearing staircase—
The step behind you is gone.
Shadows that clamor in the darkness,
Whispers rumoring a forsaken place.
Onward, onward, you are returning
A legend, a demigod, to the stars.

Shadow Song #2

The darkness always hits its mark,
Like an arrow true through the heart of man.
The song redeems not one from the darkness.
The song redeems not one from the shadows.
The grave displays an open wound to the night
And not one was saved from the shadow by light.
A truer darkness was never beheld
Than by the eye within itself.
An endless calm reigned over the shadows
Like a litany of beauty over my soul
And strange variations of a forgotten song
Played in the last resonation of a midnight bell.
The cold, and the lost, and the unredeemed
Met under a spell of starlight,
And those who felt betrayed
Opened their eyes and beheld my silence.
And the passing words I spoke
Collapsed with fire.

Shadow Song #3

In this great indisposition called my life,
All is complicit, including my shadow,
With the torturous punctuality of time.
Sometimes, like a drunk in love with his drunkenness,
I find that I cannot reconcile
The descent of the sun over the water
With death's irresistible rip-tide.
But tonight, I listen to the gasping of the sea
Unburdening its song of darkness
As the shadow of my own existence
Elongates for an eternity.

Shadow Song #8

Through this kaleidoscope of broken thoughts,
I can see a thousand dreams of the night.
The last light from the lamps on the road
Goes out with wicked laughter.
A dangerous crow is lapping up the toxic shadows
And a naked crone stalks the stars
With her gnarled cane.
A zephyr breeds with a lunatic wind in the west
And a prophet sits on the edge
Of a high cliff, reconfiguring
The constellations to his liking.
I am alone.
The moon-dagger pierces my brain
And I bleed the night.

Shadow Song #9

Panic drums the heart—
a breath close to dying
carries me down the stairs
and out into the night,
where bivouacs of a billion stars
loom near the fortress of my heart.
Livid sorghums stretch
like a nightmare-awakened gasp.
The blue moon yawns contented
in its infamy. I yawn back
as sojourners will.
Time is a madman that laughs
hysterically at our non-sequitur lives.
The liar's fate—forced to believe the lies.
Receptive to none but shadows now
I kiss oblivion and weep moonlight tears.
Nearer to death
than my freedom would have me believe,
I already wear the black mask
of a long-predetermined fate
that has also led me here,
beneath my stars.
I am blown threadbare
by a gust of cool wind
eastward in sin.
Nonsense knows its own wisdom
according to the law.

ANOTHER MISSED CONNECTION

Even the crazed seek the light
when it comes from far off.
(This light is just for me, just for me tonight.)
Cracked decanters of wisdom
sparkle in the field,
wildflowers that will not last
the foible chill of Autumn.
The moon, in full blossom,
sings its song of sweet oblivion
and I sing back in thanks
for the shadows which by tomorrow
will be gone.

Bottled Lightning

Do you hear a wind blow
through these words,
rustling them like leaves
in the high branches
before a storm?
That wind is your soul
giving itself over to mine.
There is a static born of great love.
Those who feel it
are as if struck dumb by a lightning bolt.
They walk around dazed,
unable to speak.
Their eyes are wide but they do not see.
Friends pry them with questioning,
but they have no reply. Everything is changed.
There is great electricity between you and I.
Men have braved wilder terrain than this
to satisfy their need to feel what we might feel
by the time this gust of wind subsides.
In the silence that will inevitably come,
is there space for a love such as this?
I will trust the rolling thunder
that there is.

The Saint on Top of the Mountain

Who has passed under these trees
in the ghostly light of the moon like a shaman,
incanting spells and weaving algorithms
with his hands, whispering a sly greeting
with his eye to the friendly tortoise
perched atop the purple globe light
that lines this path? Tinsel lines the path
to the top of the mountain.
It was put there by the saint that lives there.
In the bucket of rain beside the little hut,
a sprig of lavender has been placed
to mark the season of the man's soul.
Up here he bangs a gong at sunrise
and at sunset. Not for himself but for the
sun, you see, as a means to honor its eternity.
(He doesn't know that even the sun will someday die—
blessed be his naiveté. No one has the nerve to tell him.
Besides, they come to him seeking only knowledge
which he readily gives, in the form of wisdom.)
His face and hair have turned moon-white—
too thirsty for solitude, now heavy with its waters
or is it wine? Some would say he is a fool
to be so sublime, to answer every question
with a hidden gesture, a change in the eye
that one can only guess at in the dark.
"Isn't it all pretend?" I ask him, hoping to pierce his heart.
He only watches the moon, as if waiting for *it* to answer.

Daniel Senser

And there is wisdom in this, if one
can look past its foolishness.
The waiting for an answer is not pretend,
says the soul of the wise man.
It is desperate, primitive as the moon and stars.
If you stay here with me, there's no need to keep asking.
Ask once, and wait. That is enough.

Gift of Pleasure

I tasted the sweet nectar of her kiss
And, as a drunkard who's never satisfied
until he is sick,
I craved the taste of her most exotic flower—
the one that grows in her body's most hidden chamber,
the rose of her equinox,
the lotus of her paradisal waters.
She did not resist.
I placed my lips on that pink bud
and as it opened, as if to daylight,
my tongue, like the head of a charmed cobra,
immersed itself in its dance.
Such sweet sounds of delight I heard
as if I were passing the isle of Sirens
or hearing angels declaring God's word.
My eyes, which orbit her body
like moons, filled with tears and wept for joy.
Seeing this, she smiled and said:
"What's the matter? Why are you crying? Are you upset?"
"No," I replied. "It's just that,
I have never tasted anything so sweet, so rich,
so full of life! It is as if
I have torn away all the tusks of existence
and found inside the rarest of fruits,
the most luminous of gems!
Ah, to what shall I drink this sweet ambrosia
if not your flesh and all it demands?
Now lay back, my love, and let me return
to my sacred duty, the gifting of pleasure
once promised by God in creation of your beauty."

Driving While Intoxicated

How your dreary eyes sink
like stones in the hot soup of your drunkenness.
Skilled at the art of transience
you drown like a buddha
at the bottom of a lake—one bubble
of breath at a time.
Consciousness knows best.
That's what you tell yourself
when you're sober. When you drink,
The wine knows best.
It was the wine that bid you take the wheel
to drive you home—
home you know so well
from mezuzah to dog-eared tome.
But not the perpetually
reappearing and disappearing of the road.
It tells a constantly restoring lie
so sly one can be hypnotized.
And besides, the drunkenness craves oblivion.
Unconsciously, you want to sleep.
(You could never fully comprehend sleep,
not even in hindsight, whether a gift
or a thief of precious time.)
Don't sleep! Do you want to die?
The path home is narrow—
narrower than the path to sleep.
The drop to death is fast and deep.
Do you want to die? Go with the road
and read the signs. Go slow.
You have the time.

Let It Be Said

He praised joyously that which gave him joy,
Both skies of pure blue and the falling rain.
He sang to the moon and laughed with the stars,
Kissed Venus and wrestled with Mars,
And kayaked down a river of his own tears
Finding God and glory at the sea.
He listened quietly to the blossoming rose
In the heat of a summer morning.
He felt the dew beneath his toes
At the top of the hill overlooking
The green valley below. He chased a dream
Like a kite in the wind, never knowing
It was he who was being followed.

Peony Song

Sing sweet to me, oh peony,
Oh peony, pink peony.
Sing sweet to me, pink peony,
Of niceties and pleasantries.

Sing sweet to me, pink peony,
Of pink champagne and delicacies,
Stirring leaves by summer breeze,
A broad veranda by the sea,
Oh peony, pink peony.

Sing sweet to me, pink peony,
Of lover's dreams beside the sea,
Their moonlit bodies
Bound in ecstasy,
Pink peony, oh peony.

Sing sweet to me, oh peony,
Of violins so merrily
Playing chords in harmony.
Sing the call of the sea,
Oh peony, pink peony.

Sing white lace white drapes
White cake white cream.
Sing clear glasses, clear diamond,
Clear dreams.

ANOTHER MISSED CONNECTION

Sing sweet to me, my love to be,
Sing sweet to me, my love.
Sing sweet to me, oh peony,
Pink peony, my love!

Beethoven in a Storm

Exiled, banished to the promenade at dusk,
I am left to collect my thoughts in the symphony of a storm.
Lightning licks the heat so hot it cracks and oozes sound.
Flashbulb of God's filter-less photography,
by which man is apprehended from himself.
No one can say what it is it captures,
takes away, sculpts for eons, then returns in an instant
to each of our breasts.

The river's *om* is unfazed by the falling rain.
Each drop adds its own voice to the collective chant.
The storm is a symphony that wants to rise to a proper climax,
Then die like Beethoven, whose knitted brow only softened
when the clouds parted, and a little glimpse of Heaven
was revealed. Below that angelic hymnal chorus,
which we men cannot truly hear,
I watch the people begin to settle like dust
and listen to the birds sing completely devoid of fear.

The Fruit

Thunderous we roll about in ginseng kisses
and lavender caress, tongue-flesh
of rose hips bursting forth their joy
mouth a-swirl with bees and nectar,
honey gold of a lovely flower formed.
We seek no shelter from the storm
other than that which we find
in each other's arms.
Ah, to be a hermit in her cave!
Two bodies purified by love and rain.
Two minds wrestling each other's passion
with bodies that were made of dust
to glisten in rainwater and unite
like two sides of the same legume—
the fruit of all creation.

Haiku

Horizontal wisp of smoke
from the wall: cobweb
in the summer breeze.

The Vixen

Her walk, like a plucked guitar string, resonates music
Long after she is gone. Her heels click the wicked rattle
Of a desert snake, and her perfume gently pecks a kiss
On the faces of her taut admirers—lunatics to the moons
That conduct the silver tides in her wine-dark eyes.
Her black and white dress as bold as the night sky
Filled with effulgent diamonds and silver-chord stars.
Hips that sway with swift and urgent balance
On the edge of the abyss of all the prying eyes.
Like the arrow of a compass, she points northward
Through your soul, melts all the ice—you can feel it
Begin to bubble in your brain. Careful that you don't drown
On your own desire. Take only what you need from this
Astounding vision. Retain it, remember it, and never ever
Give it away.

The Color Blue

Twenty-three eagles paint the afternoon
The color blue
The color blue

Lavender shadows in a sunset swoon
The air, it cools
The air, it cools

Drop of chardonnay from a sickle moon
Venus swoons
Venus swoons

Rising heat drops its dew
Drops of blue
Drops of blue

Twenty-three eagles paint the afternoon
The color blue
The color blue

Worm on a Hook

Her eyes, like swift magicians, fooled me.
Her gaze incanted many beautiful spells
that left me locked to an expectation
that she would open her mouth
and confess her love,
but it was not to be.
Though her face was flushed,
and a smile played along her lips,
her eyes, as if possessed by an inner daemon,
left my gaze and danced about the place
in search of something that attracted her more.
Cold and beautiful goddess, you trickster
whose very gaze has the power to cast my soul
into Hell, why is it that I keep following you,
offering you my very life and being
like a wave that breaks upon the sand?
Vicious tide! Why must you pull me away?

Wake or Sleep

Thrust as one desperate cry for love
out of the shapeless eons past,
all from a whim this conflagration spread
and will continue to burn till this forest of eternity
is ash. Never will it be ash.
That is what the stars seem to say, at least.
That is the promise that is hidden in the lover's voice.
You want to know why there are shadows
moving in and out of this poem?
It is because all lovers desire a private space
to make love, and then rest.
Sleep here if you like.
Or wake, if you are sleeping.

Little-Known Facts About the Great Philosophers

Socrates got lost on the way to deliver
his Master's thesis, and lost every page
in a stiff wind. He didn't bother rewriting it.

Plato asked Socrates where the best place to
buy a gyro was. Plato
didn't include this in the Dialogues.

Diogenes lost his temper once.
He defended himself by saying
he didn't need it.

When asked to explain his concept
of the *Ubermensch*,
Nietchze stripped naked and
stood on the table, arms akimbo, saying:
"Observe, gentlemen!"

Kierkegaard once snatched a portrait
being drawn of him unsolicited
by an artist, crumpled it up,
put it in his mouth, and swallowed it.
"That will teach you to draw
a great man poorly!" he said.

A fly flew onto a piece of pecan pie
that Thomas Aquinas was eating.

Daniel Senser

When asked why he did not swat
the fly away, Aquinas said:
"The meek shall inherit the Earth,
and I want to be on their good side."

Foucault passed a group of children
playing in a park one day and smiled.
Then later he scolded himself for
taking the suppressive system of
socialization lightly.

Eternally

Await, but secretly, the perfect refuge
of the lover's embrace. Here, where Time
swallows its judgments and goes about
its business with quiet, ironical repose,
there is no room for space—our bodies
must possess one another and everything else,
every minutia of truth must be discovered
with an infinitude of kisses—here a kiss
from the blue sky, there a kiss up from the earth.
We are children hanging on to the edge of innocence.
We weep tears that become the morning dew.
Our bodies are the instruments through which
our love plays the music of our souls.
Within you, without you, it doesn't matter.
I know you now, eternally.

Conscience Absentium

Lantern-headed men gather in the night,
silently chanting and bowing their medicine
to the rabid moon.
Wicked-eyed field mice sneak from garbage mound
to garbage mound, snickering over
their own unearned privilege.
The head and tail of the squashed worm on the pavement
try to explain its pain to someone, anyone,
no one listens. Even the raven
on the tree branch is too distracted
by the worms in its belly
squirming their way toward degradation
to see. Its low caw is an exegesis
of the book of shadows. The stars want nothing more
than to use it for the propagation
of their own legends. The moon does not care.
He is rolling around and around
chasing balls inside the lottery machine
of its mind. I am in a dark room,
standing at an open window looking out at all this.
The bells chime eleven times.
Time has sway over the stillness.
Even the passing breeze cannot absolve the air
of its multiplicity of crimes.
I sigh deep, and wait long into the night
for my conscience to answer.

Sestet

Brown-skinned girl
reaching from a white canoe.
The azure-winged butterfly
flutters off into the reeds,
just beyond her grasp—
instead, catches a sunbeam.

Consumed by Flame

The pain of consumption by flame
has no trouble bridging the synaptic gap
to the place where madness
and reason converge.
Snap a man's will in half like a stick
and the sound carries on forever.
The forest is burning.
From the constant roar of its offering
birds fly, announcing escape
in the harsh guttural tones
of their worst fears realized.
Silent, a salamander creeps from the blaze.
Bright green, it stands out against the wall of flame.
Its dark eyes have seen everything:
fire's slow discovery of ash,
the stillness of a moment bound in eternity,
on the edge of a whisper—
some hissing whisper that might be flame.

Child of the Night Sky

This bottle of wine is the nipple of the moon.
Glad child of the sky, I suckle the moon-milk
And wail such that the stars hear my cry.
My adoptive mother, Earth, holds me,
But my veins are full of moonbeams,
And my tears are falling stars.
My flesh, like dust, is made of Earth,
But my soul speaks the language of the starry night.
At the break of day, my shadow reminds me
That the ache of my toil is the ache of separation
Of my eyes from my tears, and the weariness I feel
Is the weariness of a body whose blood is moonlight.

The Wound of Time

Time's blood seeps from the bodies of the bells
and flows through these streets such that we are drowning.
Each of us at the mercy of a wound that never closes,
the wound that God at the beginning created in Creation—
or was it man who stabbed the naked flesh of his being
and collectively bleeds now according to the hours?
Ah, but what is time but a stone falling from Heaven,
in a realm of eternal depth, seeking gravity and the finality
of an earthly impact? Time can't be salvaged
but perhaps with death. The long breath we take
before this plunge into life perhaps has no beginning.
Oh Lord, is there an end?

Tonight, We Dance

Tonight, we let our heads float away
into the vast blue ether,
so close to oblivion and yet so bright
and fast and fervent like the creation
of a star.

Tonight is the perfect night to play
the music of the spheres
and shape the madness into something pure
like a poem, or a string of pearls.
Man knows this night for its oblivion.
The gods, for its opportunity.
Let us be gods tonight and dance
to the rhythm of our sister, Gaia.

Tonight is the night that we have
eons to rise. Forged by stars,
our hearts become diamonds.
Like smoke from the inferno
a prayer rises from the chaos
of our lips.

Persuaded by the music, our bodies sway
to the lovelorn dance of inevitable reckoning.
Lightning runs through our veins and our steps
land like thunder. We shatter thought with

Daniel Senser

a willful blow of our desire. Lust rises
up from the veins of the Earth, igniting each step.

Our hands, in a moment of panic, search for our heads,
but they are gone. Our hands, resigned to fulfill
the pledge our souls made to the music,
rejoin the dance. Our heads don't even say goodbye.

Elegiac Romance

Our eyes explored the immutable vastness
of the star-filled sky
as our hands revisited
the cold caress of an elegiac romance
born from some forgotten shadow
in our past.

Silence loomed like seven vultures
till the dark sound of omniscient horns
echoing from mountain side to mountain side
announced our love's release.
We breathed in each other's breaths,
explored again the endless halls and chambers
of our erotic mansions, and collapsed
like drops of dew upon the grass,
breathing in and breathing out
wisps of breath in the cool early-morning dark.

A promise of romance made upon a dying star.
Again, here we are.
Lost to each other, lost in the infinite.
Is this air or darkness that we breathe?

Sanctuary of the Black Moon

We all keep a suspicious eye out
for the firebrand amidst the congregation
in the sanctuary of the black moon.

Darkness rides in on the back of a raven.
The firebrand rises on his twisted laugh.
Like the eye of a storm we sit in stupefied silence
as the unwarranted prayer begins.

In ten thousand tongues the devil is speaking.
Runes of fire written in the air above us
trace, it seems, the very paths of our souls
that led to this, our inevitable damnation.

For we have gambled away all our tears
for diamonds and laughed away all our humor
on jokes too crude to tell a mongrel dog.

Black flames of a fire born from the abyss
of Hell now rise, yet our flesh remains intact.
The flesh we worshipped remains sacred still
to God. But our souls which we let run rampant
burn with the devil's vile wrath.

Oh, how we had evaded torment in our brief
encounter with life! Had we faced even but
the inkling of pain that existed within us,

ANOTHER MISSED CONNECTION

acknowledged it as a worthy counterpart
to our lust and our greed, gave it the freedom
to refine our souls, then! Oh, then we would
have known what it was to worship, and would
now find our place among God's chosen!

Beyond the sound of the screaming damned
from somewhere outside this unholy church,
a solitary voice is heard—a young child's,
as if at play…

A Drunkard Thinks

Star-scattered and swaying,
the night collapsing to his eyes
like tender veal to teeth,
a drunkard stands upon the earth
with more weight than he can realize.
The soil is not virgin but promiscuous,
dry as dust-made bone—
a soil like a dry heave
straight from the ribs
of opinion-less death.
And long he gazes upward
from this spot like a scavenger
who makes meals of the stars.
Wading on too many thoughts,
He filters them down to a single one:

I myself am my own breed
of man, and I am dying.
No one will put me in any books.
I won't be given a Latin name.
But I will have this moment here,
and perhaps the shadows are taking note.
There's a lot of me here right now,
I'll tell you that. Though I suppose
some of me isn't.

Dawn

My shadow struck the earth and shattered
into a million butterflies at dawn.
Darkness immersed itself in an ocean of light
and found treasures there
that reflected back the stars.
I have wept such that my tears have risen up
in a cloud of mist that veiled me
shielded me from the eyes
of those whose cups I would fill
and make drunk on the sweet nectar of my song.
The cloud lifts, and, now with
the grace of a once-hidden beauty revealed,
my voice takes over where my tears left off.

Two Songbirds

This cigarette
is a sweet blaspheme whose retribution might be death.
I hear her singing with neon luminescence
in the apartment across the way,
unwinding rhapsody, reverberating hellfire,
the last gasp of nocturnal mania
before the sunrise.

A line,
"Oh, I slipped on the dock
and busted my head.
I woke up with Johnny
between my legs,"
fills me with corruptive laughter.
A vulgar muse hangs
between my thighs
so, as the milky sunlight creeps up the sky,
I sing to my neighbor
this reply:

"Johnny's got nothing
on this guy here.
By the time I'm done with you,
you'll be in tears."

Magmatic blush and silly-dumb smile
as we lock eyes from our windows,

ANOTHER MISSED CONNECTION

both of us nubile and half-naked
in the virgin-dawn light.
Two blue birds in a cherry tree,
preening and singing,
carry their carnal knowledge
with grace.

This spring morning,
I feel my heart lifting
like the sun that never grows weary
of stretching its long-limbed rays
across the amazed gasp
of space.

Pin Drop

I heard a pin drop
in the middle of the night.
It arrested my dreams
which I rode like a wave
toward oblivion.
The sound crawled into
my sheets, made them
electric, like a scorpion
it crawled into my ear.
Like an assassin
with the tiniest vial
of cyanide.
My heart leapt
from a hundred-story building,
awoke in a morgue.
Eyes opened, pierced
by a silver point.
Feet to floor, perhaps death
in this crazed search
for pin in fabric.

Swallow the Night

I walked out into the night
with the desire to swallow it whole.
Instead I swallowed many drafts
of alcohol, and let oblivion
swallow the night.

Prayer

The breath of God roars through my soul—
the all-forgiving breath of God.

Tears of reverence roll down my cheek.
I hear him speak:

Go forth now, my son, from darkness.
Discover yourself in the vast, illuminated world.

Let curiosity be your weapon,
and wisdom, your shield.

When all the shadows converge,
the stars will appear.

When the skies are overcast,
say a prayer with every step.

I will be listening.
There will always be a light.

Though the night be long,
the sun rises swiftly at dawn.

Bear witness to the wonders I have given you,
and you will bear witness to the blessedness of your own soul.

ANOTHER MISSED CONNECTION

*Remember: there is no darkness
that my light cannot overcome.*

Enlightened, I speak the word,

Amen.

On a Night Spent Dancing with a Vestal Virgin

I met her on a blue moon's night
and we danced as free and light
as raindrops on a puddle dance.

Drunken muses all around
got drunker still from the sound
of violins cavorting with
a secretly drunken God.

She whispered in my ear
that she was a vestal virgin.
I pointed at her breast and said:
"There's a fire within as well."
She sighed and lay her head against my chest,
and we danced until the fire died
and smoke met the rosy fingers of dawn.
Heavy now in my arms
she slept, and I envisioned her gentle virgin dreams.
I carried her softly to my bed
and lay her down and watched her sleep.

From the window, I could see the moon,
now chalky white and dim—
so distant, I thought, it had forgotten
the entire world.

Typhoon

He closed his eyes and sank his soul
into devastating breath that teased
the edge of silence. Tormented
by the cold objective code
of his deranged consciousness, it was only
the hellfire warmth of his long-repressed
unconscious—the strange demons
and magical runes—that calmed
his heart, as if it were so cold only
hellfire could thaw it. Demons
in a long canoe rowed across the lake
of his eyes. The beehive in his brain
dripped honey, he dreamt in sweet
honey gold. Sleeping, he could not smell
the blue typhoon ripping savage
over the mesmerized beach outside,
could not hear the dark trees as they were
twisted and wrenched like old nails
by the wind, nor the rain as it spewed
against the window pane. Only the sharp
smash of a tree limb flying through his window
woke him. The air was suddenly cool and alive.
Consciousness consumed him, pulled him away
like an irresistible rip tide.

Upon Seeing a Starlet in the Street

There she was, waltzing through the snow
on that crisp and calm December night
in her much-coveted green varnished leather boots,
the strands of her golden hair hanging
and glistening in the streetlight.

She raised her petite hand, and revealed
a gaudy diamond ring,
but before I could distinguish the exact finger,
she smiled, and waved
a prissy little wave.

Be soft, Daniel! She has no idea
who you are. She's waving at the people
behind you.

My heart unravels like a long red carpet
that leads me on to the vast, dark, and empty
movie hall—tonight, premiering my soul.

Phantoms

I stop and stare at a group of phantoms
conversing around an outdoor dining set
in the middle of the night.
Silently they chatter and consume
phantom bread and cheese.
Are they spirits? Crystalized souls
that still have an appetite
for this world?
Or are they stardust—rogue particles
illuminated just right by the streetlamp?
Or maybe I really am mad.
Surely the young woman at the window
of this old house thinks so
as she notices me leaning over the fence
staring at the empty dining set
in her yard.

Jewish Humor

I have brought a thousand souls
down to the river, promising
baptismal regeneration and
drowned every one.

Now Christ Himself wants
to return and all I can do
is say, "Bah humbug!"

I wear a Star of David
in case the Rapture comes.
Jesus wouldn't condemn
a brother to eternal damnation,
would he?

Lunacy is my excuse.
I thought I was following
God's orders.
You know, the God that
commanded Abraham
to kill his eldest son?
Guess He forgot to send
the angel this time.
I've always been a fatalist,
so you'll excuse me
when I say it was
meant to be.

ANOTHER MISSED CONNECTION

Even God would say
it's best to have
a sense of humor
about these things.
Because life is just
the punchline
to the joke
of existence,
and death the uproarious
laughter of a God
who's followed us closely
and with building suspense
wanting so desperately
to be surprised.

Ode to Watermelon

Watermelon makes me a man
filled with goodwill towards his fellow man
despite the fact that it makes my fingers sticky
and no amount of licking will do.

The whole watermelon is gone before I've had my fill.
My mother used to say, "If you eat too much watermelon,
your belly will burst!"
Just yesterday, I found myself sprawled out

in a chair in my kitchen,
wearing only boxer shorts,
my belly protruding, an entire watermelon inside.
I almost called my mother to tell her
but the groaning in my belly told me
it was better to let sleeping dogs lie.

Desert Scene

The dawn breaks
a thousand harmonic tones
across the desert sky.
A song so pure and deep
like angels mourning
a fallen star.
The sandstone structures
once unrecognized
one by one are illuminated
like rapturous supplicants
contorted in their desire.
The stars know the sun
and honor her presence
by bowing out slowly
from the morning sky.
The lunatic moon
hides its face to weep
and mourn the cessation
of its boundless gift.
The world turns and
like an echo of shadow
that once was,
the sun burns and reconciles
the breath to the soul—
the body breathless
as the mind must come to terms
with gold.

Changes

Seven restless devils wait
in the bed of our leader tonight.
Seven restless watchers wait
For a rumored promise
Made by a rumored God.
Sleep has overtaken the drunkards
Despite their best efforts to die.
The mad men huddle naked in the cold,
Their eyes like distant planets popping
From their skulls.
The thieves have stolen the key to the city.
The bureaucrats have cut out our tongues.
The priests are on hunger strike
In the tabernacle. The whores
Are locked away like precious gold.
Stories are told continuously
Without beginning and without end
By strangers at every trash can fire
On every corner of this land.
The virile have been castrated
And sing in concert halls.
The bones of missionaries lay scattered,
Chewed by mongrel dogs.
Superstition is the currency
With which we buy our bread.
Wait, don't let time deceive you.
These changes never end.

Meeting Tolstoy

One late afternoon in early autumn—
The sky was blue except for a few streaks
Of solid gray clouds near the eastern horizon—
I found myself walking on a country road
In western Russia.
To my right was a vast field, flat and green,
With a house well off in the distance.
A single dead oak, giant and formidable,
Loomed near the road.
On one of its gnarled branches were perched
Two happy blue birds, singing.
To my left was a field of grain.
My mood was pensive, and every golden blade
Seemed to hint at a greater mystery that
With every gush of wind was closer
To being unlocked.
Something was seeping slowly into my mind,
A memory from before my time,
Like a dream that beckons one to sleep,
Or ancient music soft and deep,
That carries the soul like a tide
Into an ocean of frenzied yearning.
And indeed, just then I heard such music.
It was coming from just up the road,
Where a man was mowing with an old scythe.
He was singing a song that was strange,
Yet familiar, in a voice that was deep

And wracked with a burden that was old
And unnamable.
As I approached, I studied his face.
It was unmistakable—the fierceness of his brow,
His eagle's eyes, his implacable grimace.
It was Leo Tolstoy, in the latter part of his many years.
He stopped his work and looked at me,
Sweat pouring down his brow.
He nodded his head. I bowed.
I stood like a fool, waiting for him to speak.
Modestly he looked at the ground,
Then back at me.
"You wonder why an old man like me
is out here working all alone.
I'll tell you: this grain is not my own.
It belongs to us all, especially the poor and the meek.
I work for them. This brings me peace.
So go, do your work. God gave you time and strength.
Use them well, and that will be its own reward."
I tried to reply, but a heavy wind blew in from the west.
The waves of grain gushed and the sound blocked my voice.
Because he seemed to understand,
I smiled and nodded, turned and walked away.

The Lunatic's Howl

The lunatic howls beauty
back at the moon.
The stars are electrodes
attached to the boundless firmament.
Her mind quivers with the shock
of a thousand epiphanies
all at once
dark dancing gypsies
are given free reign
over a life of pain lived freely.
Her mind is a cage—once opened,
thoughts like birds
come and go as they please.

Meanwhile, an old
gray-bearded fiddler
plays a mazurka
with his legs crossed on a cloud
as the lunatic tears
out her hair
tossing the silver tufts
up toward the moon.

About the Author

Daniel Senser is originally from Cincinnati, Ohio. He attended the University of Cincinnati where he received a BA in English. He began writing in elementary school, but started his career as a poet his freshman year of college after reading The Iliad. He was also greatly influenced by ancient Eastern poetry, the works of Jorge Louis Borges and other Hispanic writers, as well as contemporary writers such as Billy Collins and Charles Simic. Works by Daniel have been featured in such journals as: Adelaide, Jewish Currents, and California Quarterly, among others. He currently lives in Cambridge, Massachusetts.

www.ingramcontent.com/pod-product-compliance
Lightning Source LLC
Chambersburg PA
CBHW020228090426
42735CB00010B/1620